34.11/2017

Toads

Patrick Merrick

THE CHILD'S WORLD®, INC.

Library of Congress Cataloging-in-Publication Data
Merrick, Patrick.
Toads / by Patrick Merrick.
p.   cm.
Includes index.
Summary: Describes the physical characteristics,
behavior, habitat, and life cycle of toads
and explains how they differ from frogs.
ISBN 1-56766-502-0 (lib. reinforced : alk paper)
1. Toads—Juvenile literature.   [1. Toads.]   I. Title.
QL668.E227M47   1998
597.8'7—dc21   97-27838
CIP
AC

Photo Credits

ANIMALS ANIMALS © Breck P. Kent: 19
© Doug Wechsler/VIREO: 10
© 1997 Gary Meszaros/Dembinsky Photo Assoc. Inc.: cover, 2, 9, 29
© Robert and Linda Mitchell: 6, 13, 15, 16, 30
© 1994 Sharon Cummings/Dembinsky Photo Assoc. Inc.: 24
© 1997 Sharon Cummings/Dembinsky Photo Assoc. Inc.: 20, 23
© 1991 Skip Moody/Dembinsky Photo Assoc. inc.: 26

On the cover...

Front cover: This *American toad* is sitting in some moss.
Page 2: This American toad is resting near some flowers.

Toads

Table of Contents

Chapter	Page
Meet the Toad!	7
How Are Toads Different from Frogs?	8
What Do Toads Look Like?	11
Where Do Toads Live?	17
What Do Toads Eat?	18
How Are Baby Toads Born?	21
What Are Tadpoles?	25
Do Toads Have Any Enemies?	27
Are Toads in Danger?	31
Index & Glossary	32

On spring nights, you can often hear the chirps, clicks, and rumbles of the animal world. If you listen closely, you will hear a high, pretty song. What is making this sound? When you look, all you can see is some grass and some small rocks. But as you watch, one of the rocks begin to move! It's not a rock, it's one of nature's great singers. It's a toad.

How Are Toads Different From Frogs?

Toads are part of a large group of animals called **amphibians**. Amphibians are animals that spend the first part of their lives underwater. They spend the second part living on the land and breathing air. The most common amphibians are frogs and toads.

Toads and frogs are alike in many ways, but they are also different. Frogs have thin bodies with smooth, wet skin and long legs. They spend most of their lives in the water. Toads have small, fat bodies with dry skin and shorter legs. They spend most of their lives on dry land.

This American toad is sitting in a shallow pond. ⇒

Most toads are about three inches long, but some are bigger or smaller. One kind, called the *oak toad*, is only one inch long. Another kind, the *giant toad*, is almost 10 inches long! The legs of all toads are short and thick. The toads use their legs to crawl around. They hop only when they are in danger.

⇐ *Giant toads* like this one can grow very large.

The *spadefoot toad* doesn't just use its feet to move around. It uses them to dig backwards into the ground! It digs a **burrow**, or underground home, where it stays for a few weeks. It comes out of its burrow only when it is wet or rainy.

This *spadefoot toad* has buried itself in the sand. ⇒

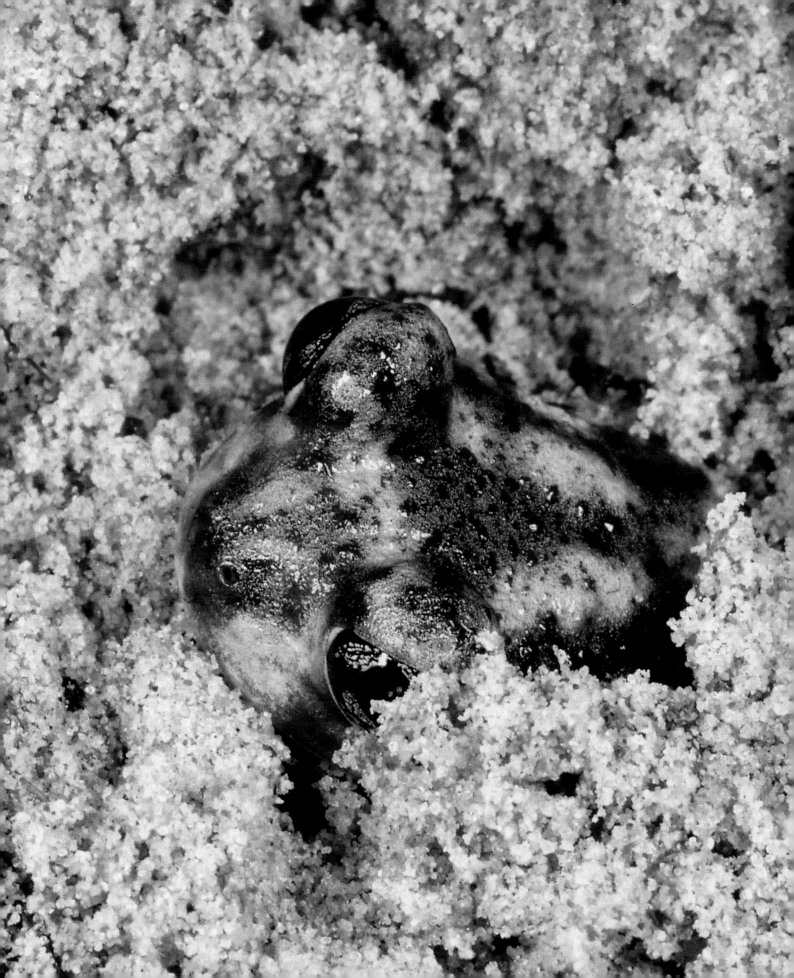

Toads have large eyes. They can see very well on land and in the water. They also have excellent hearing. A toad's ears look like dark circles on the sides of its head. These ears can hear the sound of faraway footsteps—even when the toad is in the middle of a pond!

Toads' dry skin comes in lots of colors. It also has large bumps called *warts*. For a long time, people thought you could get warts by touching a toad. This is not true. You cannot get warts by touching a toad.

This *Asiatic toad* is resting near some plants. ⇒

Toads live almost everywhere in the world except near the North and South Poles. But they like warm, moist places the best. That is because toads are **cold-blooded**. That means their bodies cannot make their own heat. If a toad gets too cold, it could freeze to death. To stay alive, the toad **hibernates**, or goes into a deep sleep, until warmer weather comes.

Most toads do not like the sun because it dries out their bodies. If their bodies lose too much water, the toads die. Because of this, most toads are **nocturnal**— they only come out at night. In the dark, the toads can eat and move around without drying out their bodies.

⇐ This *marine toad* is trying to hide in a hollow tree.

What Do Toads Eat?

Toads are **predators**. Predators are animals that hunt and eat other animals. Toads hunt mostly insects. They will also eat such things as earthworms. Toads will only eat creatures that are alive and moving. If an insect or worm sits very still, a toad will not eat it. But if it moves, it's toad food!

Toads can eat a lot. One toad can eat almost 100 flies in 10 minutes! The toad catches most of its food on the end of its long, sticky tongue. But toads do not have teeth. Instead, they swallow their food alive and whole.

This American toad is eating an earthworm. ⇒

How Are Baby Toads Born?

When a male toad sings, he is calling to female toads. The louder he sings, the more likely he is to find a mate. To make a big sound, the male toad puffs air into a huge **vocal sac** under his chin. When the sac is full, he can make a loud noise.

⇐ This male American toad is filling its vocal sac with air.

After the toads mate, the female lays up to 30,000 soft, clear eggs. Most toads leave their eggs in long rows underwater. The eggs are always in danger of being eaten. Fish and other animals love toads' eggs. The *midwife toad* has found a way to keep its eggs safe. Midwife toads don't leave their eggs behind. They carry them on their backs until the eggs are ready to hatch!

These eggs will grow into hundreds of American toads. ⇒

Some toad eggs hatch in one day. Others take a few weeks to hatch. What comes out of a toad egg does not look like a toad. It is a **tadpole**. A tadpole is a baby toad, but it looks like a tiny fish. The tadpole lives in the water and changes as it grows. After a few weeks, it begins to grow legs and breathe air. Later, its back legs get longer and its tail shrinks. Then it is time for the tadpole to leave the water and live on land.

⇐ This American toad tadpole still has a very long tail.

Do Toads Have Any Enemies?

Birds, snakes, and many other animals like to eat toads. But toads have found ways to protect themselves. Most toads have **camouflage** that helps them hide. Camouflage is coloring that blends in with rocks and grasses. This camouflage makes the toads very hard to find.

⇐ This American toad is hard to see when it sits on dead leaves.

Other toads puff themselves full of air or show their brightly colored bellies. This makes the toads look bigger and scarier. Some toads even use poison to stay safe. The American toad has a poison on its back that tastes terrible. Animals that try to eat the toad quickly spit it out! Other toads have very dangerous poisons. You should always wash your hands after touching a toad.

American toads like this one protect themselves with poison. ⇒

Many toads die from pollution of the water and soil in which they live. Farming and building destroys many other toads' homes. As toads die, the animals that eat them begin to disappear, too. Without toads, there would be many more insects such as flies and mosquitoes to bother us. To help the toads, we must all work to reduce pollution. If we can protect the toads and their homes, we'll hear the toad's beautiful voice for many springs to come.

⟵ This *Malayan spotted toad* has beautiful colors.

Glossary

amphibians (am–FIH–bee–uhnz)
Amphibians are animals that spend the first part of their lives in the water and the second part on land. Toads and frogs are amphibians.

burrow (BUR–oh)
A burrow is a hole an animal digs for shelter. Spadefoot toads dig burrows with their back feet.

camouflage (KAM–uh–flazh)
Camouflage is coloring that makes an animal look like its surroundings. Many toads have camouflage that hides them.

cold-blooded (KOLD BLUH–ded)
Animals that are cold-blooded cannot warm their own bodies. Toads are cold-blooded.

hibernate (HY–bur–nate)
When animals hibernate, they go into a very long, deep sleep. Some toads hibernate during cold weather.

nocturnal (nok –TUR–null)
Animals that are nocturnal are active only at night. Most toads are nocturnal.

predators (PREH–duh–terz)
Predators are animals that kill other animals for food. Toads are predators that eats insects.

tadpole (TAD–pohl)
Tadpoles are baby toads. At first tadpoles look like little fish, but slowly they change into toads.

vocal sac (VOH–kull SAK)
A vocal sac is a pouch under a male toad's chin. The male uses its vocal sac to call to females.

Index

amphibians, 8

appearance, 8, 11, 14

burrow, 12

camouflage, 27

cold-blooded, 17

dangers to, 31

different kinds, 11-12, 22

eating, 18

eggs, 22

enemies, 27

food, 18

hibernation, 17

location, 17

movement, 11

nocturnal, 17

predators, 18

protection, 27-28

sounds, 7, 21

tadpole, 25

vocal sac, 21

warts, 14

young, 22, 25